Gross History

Gross FACTS About VIKINGS

BY MIRA VONNE

CAPSTONE PRESS
a capstone imprint

Blazers is published by Capstone Press,
1710 Roe Crest Drive, North Mankato, Minnesota 56003.
www.capstonepub.com

Library of Congress Cataloging-in-Publication Data
Names: Vonne, Mira, author.
Title: Gross facts about Vikings / by Mira Vonne.
Description: North Mankato, Minnesota : Capstone Press, [2017] | Series:
  Blazers. Gross history | Includes bibliographical references and index. |
  Audience: Grades 4-6.
Identifiers: LCCN 2016032453 (print) | LCCN 2016033195 (ebook) | ISBN
  9781515741589 (library binding) | ISBN 9781515741756 (pbk.) | ISBN
  9781515741817 (eBook PDF)
Subjects: LCSH: Vikings—Juvenile literature. | Vikings—Social life and
  customs—Juvenile literature.
Classification: LCC DL66 .V65 2017 (print) | LCC DL66 (ebook) | DDC
  948/.022—dc23
LC record available at https://lccn.loc.gov/2016032453

Editorial Credits
Mandy Robbins, editor; Philippa Jenkins, designer; Wanda Winch, media researcher;
Steve Walker, production specialist

Photo Credits
Bridgeman Images: © Look and Learn/Private Collection/English School, cover, © Look and
Learn/Private Collection/Oliver Frey, 13, © Look and Learn/Private Collection/Peter Jackson, 9,
Photo © O. Vaering/Private Collection/Peter Nicolai Arbo, 29; Capstone, 16-17; Granger, NYC – All
rights reserved/Sarin Images, 15; JORVIK Viking Centre, York Archaeological Trust for Excavation
& Research, 21; National Geographic Creative: Michael Hampshire, 11; Newscom: akg-images,
5, Photoshot/Martin Zwick, 25; North Wind Picture Archives: Gerry Embleton, 7; Science Source:
Mikkel Juul Jensen, 23; Shutterstock: irin-k, fly design, Juan Gaertner, 27, Milan M, color splotch
design, monkeystock, grunge drip design, Protasov AN, weevil, lice, parasites, Spectral-Design, 8;
Thinkstock: Dorling Kindersley, 19

Essential content terms are **bold** and are defined on the page where they first appear.

Printed and bound in China

9941S17RRD

TABLE OF CONTENTS

Raiders From the Sea

The Vikings terrorized Europe for nearly 300 years. These raiders from Scandinavia attacked anywhere they could sail. Their ships would appear without warning. They **looted** towns and captured thousands of slaves.

loot—to take treasure from a ship or town

Gross Fact

A single Viking ship could carry about 24 heavily armed warriors. Often there was more than one ship in a raid.

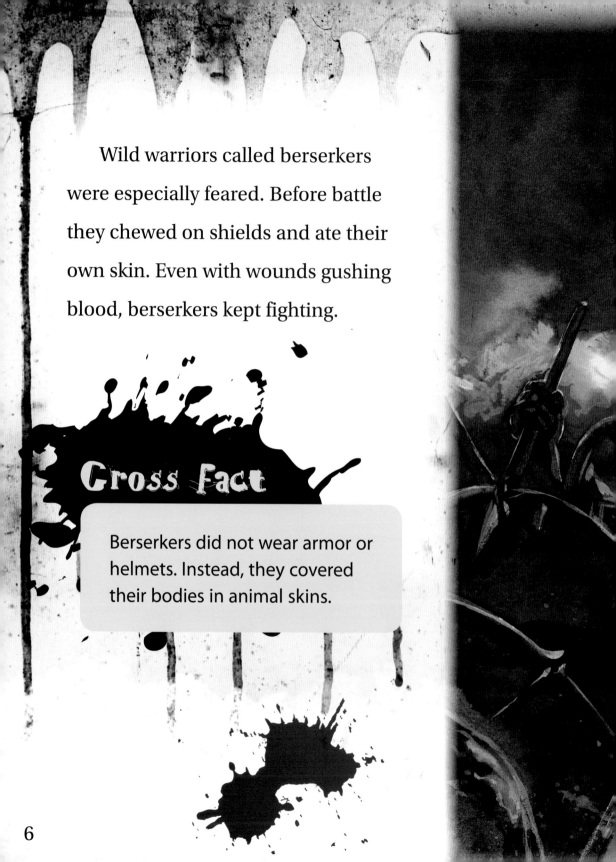

Wild warriors called berserkers were especially feared. Before battle they chewed on shields and ate their own skin. Even with wounds gushing blood, berserkers kept fighting.

Gross Fact

Berserkers did not wear armor or helmets. Instead, they covered their bodies in animal skins.

Terrible Attacks

Vikings often faced well-armed enemies. Wounds were nasty and deadly. Iron swords sliced at chests, arms, and legs. A strong blow from a sword or **battle-ax** could split a person's head open.

battle-ax—a weapon consisting of a wooden handle with a heavy, sharp blade on one end

Some Vikings would celebrate a victory with a feast on the battlefield. They set up their cooking fires among dead bodies. The fire cooked their food over the burning bodies of their enemies.

Tough Travels

Travel on Viking **longships** was tough. Warriors had no protection from the weather. Constantly being hit with seawater made skin break out in sores. The salty water stung and kept the sores from healing.

> **longship**—a long wooden boat that could be powered by sail or oar

Gross Fact

Crews spent long hours bailing out water from their ships. Sometimes their efforts weren't enough. Many Viking ships sank.

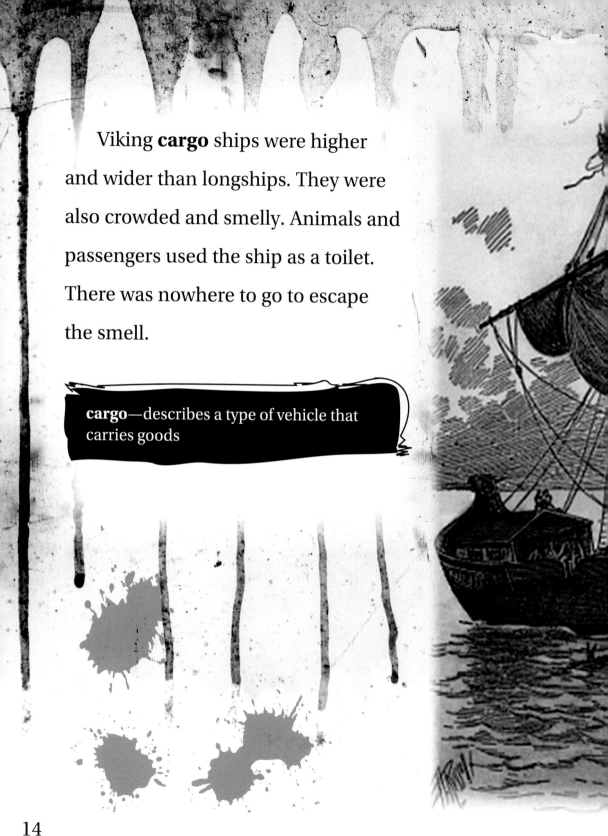

Viking **cargo** ships were higher
and wider than longships. They were
also crowded and smelly. Animals and
passengers used the ship as a toilet.
There was nowhere to go to escape
the smell.

cargo—describes a type of vehicle that
carries goods

15

The food onboard could be as rough as the seas. Nothing was cooked. The risk of starting a fire on a wooden ship was too great. Tough dried meat was washed down with **lukewarm** water or sour milk.

lukewarm—just slightly warm

Viking Homes

Vikings didn't spend all their time at sea. Most of them lived in one-room farmhouses. There were no windows. A hole in the roof let out some of the smoke from cooking fires. But the house was dark, smoky, and smelly.

Gross Fact

The Vikings themselves added to the smell. They only bathed about once a week.

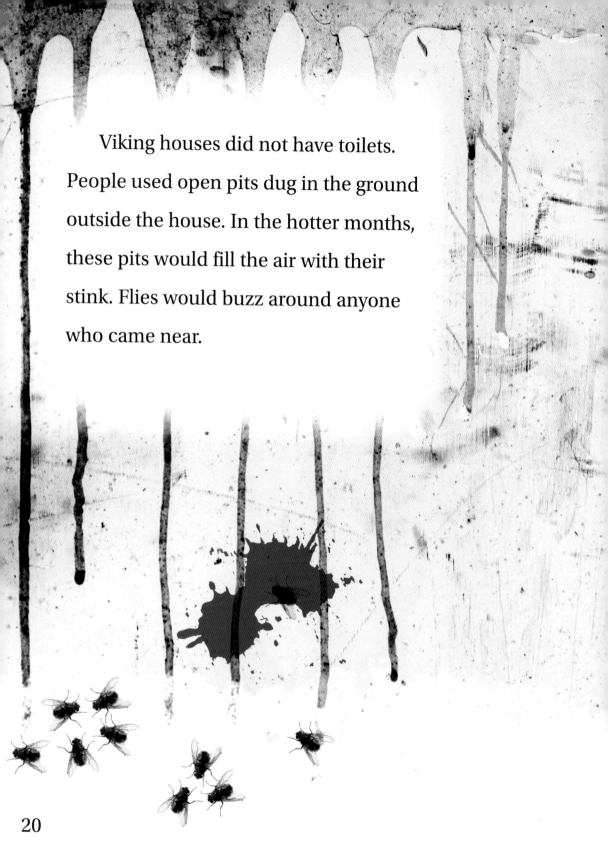

Viking houses did not have toilets. People used open pits dug in the ground outside the house. In the hotter months, these pits would fill the air with their stink. Flies would buzz around anyone who came near.

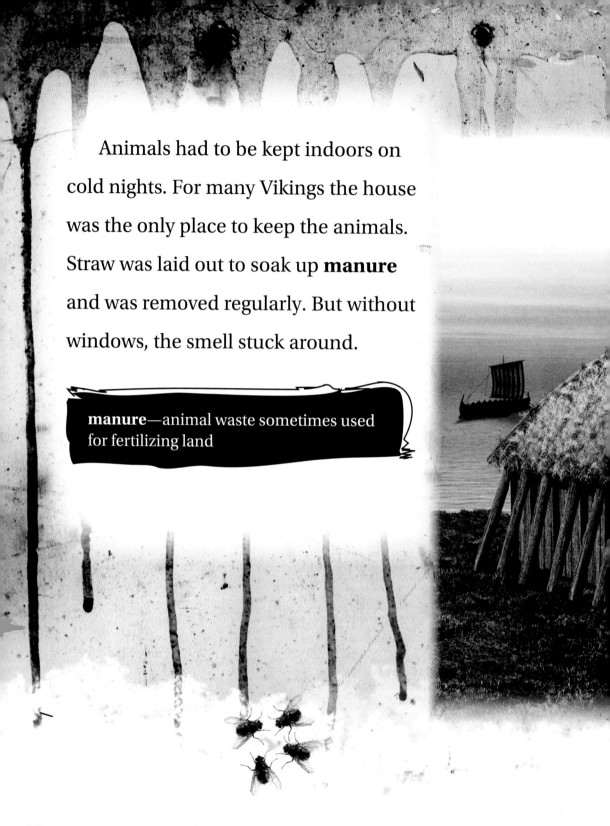

Animals had to be kept indoors on cold nights. For many Vikings the house was the only place to keep the animals. Straw was laid out to soak up **manure** and was removed regularly. But without windows, the smell stuck around.

manure—animal waste sometimes used for fertilizing land

A Sour Supper

Vikings often **fermented** their meat. Doing this kept **bacteria** from growing. It made food last longer too. Vikings would bury an animal in a pit and leave it to sour. Shark meat and whale blubber were commonly used.

ferment—to preserve food in a way that prevents organisms from growing

bacteria—very small living things that exist all around you and inside you; some bacteria cause disease

Gross Fact

The national dish of Iceland is fermented shark meat called hákari. It was a staple of the Viking diet.

Painful Problems

Vikings had no doctors. To stop bleeding, they rolled hot iron over wounds. This painful process prevented **infection**. Other health threats were lice, fleas, and tapeworms. Tapeworms caused illness and even brain damage.

infection—disease caused by germs

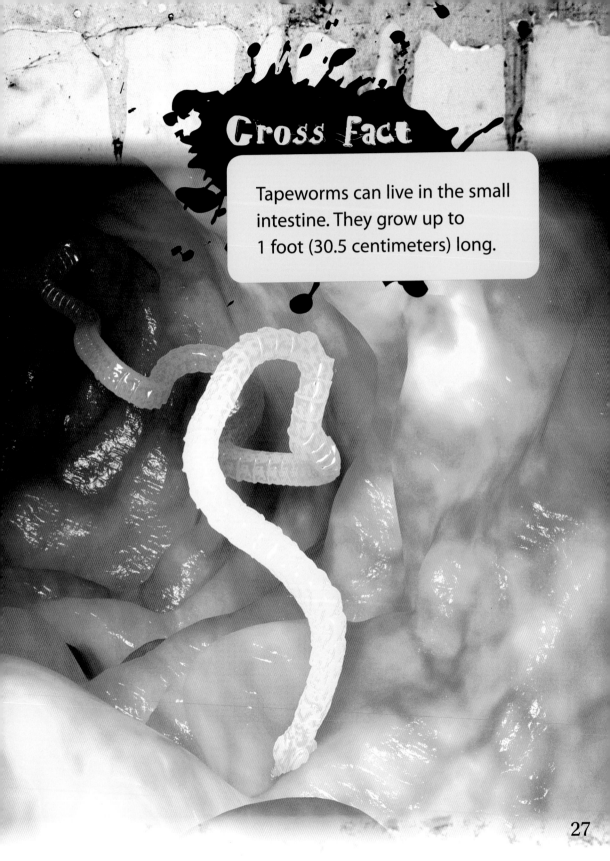

Gross Fact

Tapeworms can live in the small intestine. They grow up to 1 foot (30.5 centimeters) long.

The End of the Viking Age

In the 1060s European countries built stronger armies to fight the Vikings. It grew harder for the Vikings to raid villages. Many settled down to farm and trade. Eventually the violent Viking way of life died out.

Glossary

bacteria (bak-TEER-ee-uh)—very small living things that exist all around you and inside you; some bacteria cause disease

battle-ax (BAT-uhl-aks)—a weapon consisting of a wooden handle with a heavy, sharp blade on one end

cargo (CAR-go)—describes a type of vehicle that carries goods

ferment (fur-MENT)—to preserve food in a way that prevents organisms from growing

infection (in-FEK-shun)—disease caused by germs

longship (LONG-ship)—a wooden boat that could be powered by sail or oar

loot (LOOT)—to take treasure from a ship or town

lukewarm (LUKE-warm)—just slightly warm

manure (muh-NYOOR)—animal waste sometimes used for fertilizing land

Scandinavia (skan-duh-NAY-vee-uh)—northern European countries including Norway, Sweden, Denmark, and sometimes Finland, Iceland, and the Faeroe Islands

Read More

Higgins, Nadia. *National Geographic Kids: Everything Vikings.* Washington, D.C.: National Geographic, 2015.

Langley, Andrew. *You Wouldn't Want to be a Viking Explorer!: Voyages You'd Rather Not Make.* You Wouldn't Want To Be. New York: Franklin Watts, 2014.

Thompson, Ben. *Guts and Glory: The Vikings.* New York: Little, Brown and Company, 2015.

Internet Sites

FactHound offers a safe, fun way to find Internet sites related to this book. All of the sites on FactHound have been researched by our staff.

Here's all you do:

Visit *www.facthound.com*

Type in this code: 9781515741589

Check out projects, games and lots more at
www.capstonekids.com

Critical Thinking Using the Common Core

- The details in this book are gross. What other words can you use to describe this period in history? (Key Idea and Details)

- How do the images add information about the Vikings? Describe some of these images. (Craft and Structure)

- Compare living during the time of the Vikings with living today. Would you want to live during the 1000s? Why or why not? (Integration of Knowledge and Ideas)

Index